POEMS FROM THE THRESHOLD

Poems from the Threshold

by

Charles Entrekin

HIP POCKET PRESS
Orinda, California
2024

Also by Charles Entrekin

POETRY

What Remains (Poetic Matrix Press, 2020)

The Art of Healing (with Gail Rudd Entrekin)
(Poetic Matrix Press, 2016)

Portrait of a Romance (Hip Pocket Press, 2014)

Listening (Poetic Matrix Press, 2010)

In This Hour (Berkeley Poets Workshop & Press, 1999)

Casting for the Cutthroat & Other Poems
(Berkeley Poets Workshop & Press, 1986)

Casting for the Cutthroat (Thunder City Press, 1978)

All Pieces of a Legacy
(Berkeley Poets Workshop & Press, 1977)

PROSE

The Berkeley Poets Cooperative: A History of the Times 1968-1991
(Hip Pocket Press, 2013)

Red Mountain, Birmingham, Alabama, 1965
(El Leon Literary Arts, 2008)

Published by Hip Pocket Press
5 Del Mar Court
Orinda, CA 94563
www.hippocketpress.org

This edition was produced for on-demand distribution by
lightningsource.com for Hip Pocket Press.

Cover photo: Gail Entrekin
Author photo: Steve Haimovitz
Book design: Wayne Smith

Printed in the United States of America.

ISBN: 978-0-917658-488

Typeset in 11 point Minion
Minion Pro is an Adobe Original typeface designed by Robert
Slimbach. The first version of Minion was released in 1990. Minion Pro
is inspired by classical, old style typefaces of the late Renaissance,
a period of elegant, beautiful, and highly readable type designs.

Table of Contents

Gail, my wife and my dreamboat,
who always takes me in
when I wash ashore.

On Going Blind

*Any life, no matter how long and complex it may be, is made
up of a single moment — the moment in which a man finds
out, once and for all, who he is.*
   —Jorge Luis Borges

Alone, in a world of sensations,
sneakers on asphalt, whisper
of tires on wet pavement,
birdsong, a goldfinch trilling,
mist and sun on my face, cold
breeze under a soft March sky,
trees dripping, Spring drizzle
on my hands.

Oh, the ease of it, the comfort
of all this weather washing
over me. Traveling through
weather while blind is like
navigating by starlight.

I walk past the grocery
feeling for obstacles, cracks
in the sidewalk, with my red-
tipped cane. My blind stick finds
steps, three steps up
into the cafe.

A stranger I can almost see
opens the door to let me in.
Warm air rushes against my face,
and there is laughter, tangled
conversation, a confusion
of voices rising and falling, faint
piano music through speakers,
and two giggling children scamper
around my knees. I try not to lose

my balance as I step gingerly
to the counter and order a latte:
one honey, no foam.

I hold up my phone, tell
the barista I can't find
the scanner. She takes my hand,
guiding me to it. Her soft
electric touch against my skin
is almost overwhelming,
shocking in its immediacy,
its tenderness. A sudden
intake of breath. I am so
grateful, I want to cry.

Details

*What can be said at all can be said clearly; and whereof one
cannot speak thereof one must be silent*
—Tractatus Logico-Philosophicus *by Ludwig Wittgenstein*

These days my life is being distilled into details.
The clutter falls away because the present
demands I stay determinedly aware.
I remember to get my balance
before stepping forward into the motion of walking,
remember to swing my arms.
I have to stretch out a hand into empty space
to avoid a wall,
or wear a cap with a bill
to protect against a low-hanging branch.
I have to remember to speak with intention,
take a breath, plan what I say.

Remember to blink.

Details can become a comfort:
my hand finding the banister
that I think is there,
or feeling my kitchen chair, sliding it out,
easing down carefully,
keeping cushions from slipping away,
getting my feet under the table,
touching my plate, napkin, glass.

When I am located,
a relief settles over me.
I feel a riff of confidence, a moment of grace,
and I can begin to eat.

When the gap between
intention and reality shrinks
I am on a roll,

like a musician who knows the tune
when I find the familiar rhythm.

I can even bring a poem into the world.

I used to write to discover who I was,
hardly noticing my fast, two-fingered typing.

Now I compose, sit and think,
dictate my thoughts,
ask to play them back,
listen to my language,
change it,
dictate again,
play back,
listen more,
edit and shape,
dictate, playback, listen, share,
discovering the being I am becoming

April 1, 2019, Gratitude Poem

I find myself grateful
for the vision I have left,
to see color again
while showering –
a washcloth
suddenly appearing before me
in fulgent yellow.

Grateful to taste the food
sparkling on my tongue,
dancing highlights
of unfamiliar odors and spices,
which I can swallow
without coughing.

Grateful for the words
crawling about in my veins
as I sit with a poem in my mind
and turn it over and over
until the words fit
and do not lose
their music or magic.

Grateful to visit with friends
while the present disappears,
and explore whole worlds of new ideas
that manage to march
across the palimpsest of our minds
into comprehension and alignment.

Grateful to sit with family
around the firepit
amidst the orange trees
in my Sky Garden,
to converse one-on-one,

when the distracting world
is not intruding.

Grateful to lie beside my wife
lifted out over the horizon
of our pillows and sheets
and feel her body tremble
with anticipation,
with touching.

Grateful to discover
in a new-found friend,
a love of sharing the difference
between what is real and what is not
in a comforting office
under the blessing
and watchful gaze
of a fragmented mask of Buddha
and a Devonian fossil of a fish.

When all we have
is this fragile appreciation
of a willingness
to love and be loved,
when whatever we have
we hold between us,
as easy as walking down a street
in the untrammeled sunshine.

Esse Est Percipi
(*Experiencing Charles Bonnet Syndrome*)

To be is to be perceived.
   —*Bishop George Berkeley*

Removing the Bandages

A canopy of white guy wires
sweeps skyward as we cross the new Bay Bridge
into San Francisco.
I cannot see the Ferry Plaza,
the Transamerica Pyramid,
gray Embarcadero monoliths
reflecting stark afternoon light.
I listen to the rhythmic thrum of tires.
Instead of the cityscape, my brain creates
leafless winter trees
rising over open meadows
floating past the car window:
highway to Tuscaloosa,
Alabama winter-green grass going brown.
I know this image is all wrong.
But the grass sways with the motion of the car.

Returning Home

Winding up the two-lane road
past the California landscape:
manzanita, bay, live oak, and evergreen.
I remember leafy shadows, evening light.
But I see the tall red-brick tenements
stretching up 14th Street, NYC,
Lower East Side, 1970,
as far as my eye can see.
Where do they come from?
The buildings waver, remain following me
around the curve, over the creek.

As we drive on, the mirage
disappears in oncoming headlights.
I am learning to make friends with what I see.
Not what's there.

What Remains

Our orange cat, Scout,
too old to hunt, sits in the sun,
watches birds at the feeder.

Brown towhees ignore her.

Some days I lose my words
and my vision blurs. I am
watching bright yellow tulips unfolding,

like a loose woman
with her arms outstretched
petals limp with opening.

My hand, bumpy with skin cancers,
shakes from an unconscious tremor.
I can stop it when I try.

I want to speak how
I am disorganizing and
diminishing by degrees.

So many balls in the air
I can't catch or find, still spinning
in the lost, and the found

is what remains
like the splash of a leaping fish,
a sound rippling in the night air

and dissipating in the dew-laden dusk.

Acknowledging Parkinson's

...[T]he limits of language (of that language which I
alone understand) mean the limits of my world.
—Ludwig Wittgenstein

I used to ignore it,
a blinking red light I drove past
without stopping.

The tremor
is like a squirrel crossing the road,
indecisive,
running left, then right,

an ant
that has lost the scent,
no way to get back to the nest,
wandering aimlessly
across the unmapped countertop.

A rebellion is going on,
a soldier gone AWOL,
breaking ranks,
risking the whole,

a computer virus,
a threat to my identity
stealing my passwords,
making decisions
without me.

I try to delete it
but it comes back on its own.

In my lucid dreams,
I am unsure
who is in control.

A woman wearing bright red lipstick
offers a taste of something
dripping from her outstretched fingers.
I see her coming forward,
inviting,
but suddenly know
she is not real.
She stops,
fragmenting, shimmering,
disorganizing.

I stare but do not see her,
lost in the unrelenting
flow of sensations,
in the trembling
of the universe around her.

Exquisite

        My boys and I chat
easy time talking
tossing a football
running and catching
a green lawn
the crisp light
a summer afternoon.
        The ball is passed and
suddenly I have to react –
dive, reach and catch –
cradle a leather ball
in my right hand 'til
off balance, falling,
I let go and
throw a perfect spiral.
        It is a thing of beauty.
It takes on a life of its own.
The sight fills me with joy:
football spinning in sunlight.
        Startled awake
as the ball floats away
I rise in darkness,
my bedside lamp
shattered on the floor.

In My Backyard

Freedom, joy or bliss doesn't come from the situation that
we think we should be [in], but it derives from the one that
we are already in.
    —Aditya Ajmera

I am ensconced in the shade of the pergola,
under the arbor of flowers, brushing away
Cecile Brunner roses and wisteria vines
fighting it out for dominance.
I worry the wisteria will soon try to take over
and pull the whole thing down.

I hear a sigh of relief from my daughter-in-law,
flushed and blooming, 36 weeks pregnant.
How's the water? I ask.
It takes the weight off my back.
The pool water buoys the bounty of her burden for a short time.

Three-year-old Skylar leaps in beside her mother,
tittering in her water wings,
her splash too small to reach me on the deck.

Grandsons six- and nine-years-old
cannonball into the deep end of the pool.
No! No! No! Jess shouts. *Stop that!*
One more time and you'll have to get out!

I hear dogs' nails click on the pavement, chasing each other,
running in circles like the kids are forbidden to do,
the retriever jumping in to retrieve toys on command.

Gail sits next to me,
offers me an ice water or beer or wine
or Fritos, should I want to take a risk
of getting a coughing fit due to Parkinson's.
I settle for ice water.

She hands it to me with two hands,
placing the glass, patting me gently.

I listen to the mayhem,
squeal and splash of wrestling boys,
and I retreat into myself,
go on drift about Ibrutinib,
the targeted therapy so successful
at rendering my cancer quiescent.
It blocks the B enzymes
and the vaccine.
I have no antibodies to Covid-19.

The dogs shake their wet fur over me.

Now is the time to listen to the buzzing of bees,
the chorus of voices of my grown sons
talking basketball scores, politics,
the latest outrage on TV,
settle in to appreciate a breeze riding down
over the mountain from the ocean,
cooling, refreshing, free,
enjoy each moment as it expands
here in the shade of the pergola.

Sons Caleb and Nathan and Demian take turns
with the dogs and the kids and me,
their concern a protective sphere against
what could go wrong.

Blind Man's Walk on a Summer Morning

Today there are 3,574,262 U.S. Covid-19 cases, resulting in the loss of 139,567 American lives (July 15, 2020).

My world gets smaller and smaller. The pandemic takes away reaching out, shaking hands, touching family, hugging friends. Shelter-in-place is a surreal sequestration. I have no way to normalize this news.

I like to take my coffee outside in the morning. I find my way out the French doors, feet on the flagstones, touch the post I know, step over the hose left haphazardly across the path. With no depth perception, foreground and background get displaced. I sense an outline, visually vague. I reach for it long before I get there. When I touch the white wicker chair, it comes into view. I touch each arm, lower myself into its cushions and there is a comfort in knowing I am located.
The confirmation of what I feel fills me with gratitude.

A distant fog bank accumulates on the mountaintop, obscures Tilden Park. I know this because the coolness of the morning breeze carries a slight salt scent of ocean. I listen to the birds—mockingbirds, crows, a late robin warbling in the distance, and the tintinnabulation of the glass wind chime and then, further away, the mellow Woodstock chimes.

Sound, light, and shadow, touch, are my primary senses. I feel good about touching things. Touch is my pleasure. Even color shows up when I touch it: red dot on the TV remote, a red flower, the metal stair rail already warm. I feel secure when I touch it as I climb the stairs.

Look at the butterflies on this bush. I can't find the butterflies or the bush until Gail walks over and points to it. I see a slight movement. I ask, *What kind of flowers?*
Oregano, she answers, *I planted them last year.* Suddenly I see what passes for purple.

The virus is raging, surging, the Governor is rolling everything back, shutting the state down.

Isolation, fear of the unknown, anonymous face shields, thousands on ventilators communicating with blinks and nods, saying goodbyes on tablets.

I feel my way out of the rising noontime sun into the insulated cool of the living room. My eyes don't adjust right away. It is only dark. From the glass wind chime hanging in the nearby apple tree, a spillage of notes washes over me

Parkinson's Dream

In my vivid dream
somebody throws me a ball.
My dream friends –
young, energetic –
can throw it, catch it,
don't understand.
I try to catch it, but I can't.
I know from other dreams
I won't be able to touch it.
I don't have to catch it.

Suddenly we are at a cliff,
craggy outcroppings over ocean depths.
My companions leap from rock to rock,
laughing and then diving, one-by-one
off the cliff into the water,
urging me on.

I know they will surely die,
they are so careless
they will be killed when they hit.
But each figure enters the water safely
far below. They are only dream people
swimming away in the surf just fine.
None of it is real.
I can't do it because it isn't real.

Getting out of bed,
I shuffle across the sea of carpet,
soft as sand.
In my bedroom,
the crags and the ocean waves remain.
Touching my chest of drawers
I am brought home,
back into my body,
awake and alone.

A New Kind of Love

Matins

The daily ritual starts at 7:00.
You go off to work on your journal.
I stay in bed until 7:30.
Then you help me, now unsighted,
get out of bed,
take my hands,
lead me toward my soft chair
stuffed with pillows.

For a moment we stand naked and embrace
holding each other,
wobbly and unstable,
belly-to-belly together.

Stomach pains, unable to eat or sleep—
you haven't felt right for over a month now.
I worry and feel tender toward you.
I expect to reach out and help,
make a difference.
I am knocked back a bit finding I cannot.
Still we go forward
stepping into the shower and then getting dressed,
awkwardly, with great difficulty,
but successfully.

Vespers

Now it's 8:30 or 9:00 o'clock at night,
I am struggling
with internal Parkinson's tremors,
a jittery lack of control.
We return to the bedroom.
Changing into pajamas

we bid each other our hopes
for a peaceful night, hugging.
I'm here if you need me,
once again centering,
pressing our bellies together,
locating each other
before sleep.

Hallucinations

We are such stuff as dreams are made on
  —William Shakespeare

All are but parts of one stupendous whole/Whose body
nature is, and God the soul...
  —Alexander Pope (quoted from The Sixth Extinction
    by Elizabeth Kolbert)

I can no longer pretend
to wake and know
which way to go.
I sit on the edge of the bed,
taking it slow.

Place one foot on the floor
and then the other,
step into the luminosity
of a dream world
I can't escape,
because I am old and alone
and awake in my sleep.

I am drawn
to bright eyes in the gloom,
unsettling and cold:
Victorian dream folk
sleeping on shelves
like dolls seeing the future,
unable to speak,
a story not revealed,
something untold.

Another world in my bedroom,
a dark augury.
If I get too close,
I may be lured,

a traveler between worlds,
caught in a dream
within a dream
with nowhere to go,
loss of structure,
loss of control.

When I stand,
I am nowhere in my room.
I am in their world,
surrounded by people
who live in my dreams.

Elaine's Nails

Touch Deprivation: As more Americans are vaccinated against
Covid-19… hugging is the main event.
  —LA Times

I take a carbidopa-levodopa
to control my tremor,
think about the words from last night's sangha
on the ride down the hill.

Blind in the too-bright sunlight,
I take my friend Heidi's elbow,
enter the premises,
sit in the appointed spa chair,
hand off my shoes and socks.

It's hard to trust my stability,
unsighted, in such situations.

The absolute is what is perceived
without labels or filters.
I dip my cold feet
into the warming water.
The pedicurist turns on the jets
in the porcelain bowl.
I soak in Epsom salts
and scented oil.

Recognizing Elaine's distant voice
as she hangs up the phone,
I shout *Congratulations!*
for her shop having survived
the Covid-19 shutdown.

The pedicurist lifts my left foot
out of the water,
begins to clip my nails,

which haven't been trimmed in over two months.
They are cracked and broken,
ragged to the touch.
She slips my left foot back into the water.
It feels so clean.
She taps the right one for me to lift.

The immediacy of the moment
comes completely clear to me with her touch.
I am fully awake.

She lifts each foot gently,
one by one,
scrubs the soles,
a slight ticklish feeling on my instep,
she pumices the calluses on my heels.

Next I hear her
rubbing her palms together,
warming the oil.
She massages my toes, arches, ankles,
strong and gentle thumbs
up my calves,
first the left,
then the right.

The pedicurist and I
do not speak the same tongue.
She is Vietnamese.
Our common language is touch,
open heart,
warmth of water,
kind hands,
knowing acupressure.

Not confined in tight shoes,
relaxed,
released,
O happy feet.

Located in a Trip I Did Not Take to Slovenia
Ljubljana: 46.0569° N, 14.5058° E; Orinda: 37.8771° N, 122.1797° W

*Space is not an empirical concept which has been
derived from outer experiences.*
—Emmanuel Kant

In Slovenia my wife and son
are visiting my daughter's family,
having a good time.

I am not there.

They are nine hours ahead.
They send me digital images
that I can't see
but I appreciate and treasure.
I see them in my mind. I see what they see.
Words spin out in metaphors of landscape and love.

Ben summits Triglav,
hikes a ridge,
traverses a hanging bridge,
sees fog on an Alpine lake
and hears voices rise up in song
from a village far below.

Katy and Mitja and baby Matej,
Gail and Ben picnicking
in the yard at the cabin
on the lake in Bohinj.
Cowbells,
Albert the kitten fearlessly stalking grazing cattle,
cows fleeing.

Everything is changing.
I am close to traveling in time.
Gail speaks of the wedding and baby Matej.

I feel I can be in two places at once,
which makes my position unique.
I feel loose and floating free from attachments.
I am a unique part of the whole. I am no self.
No one can occupy this location except me.

I was thinking how I could calculate
my absolute position.
Then I realized in space-time,
I must take in the fact I am moving.
I am on Earth, which is rotating.
And this planet is bending around the sun.
And the sun, with all its worlds,
is spinning in empty space in the Milky Way.

Then it occurs to me: my location is not in physics
but in my sense of touch.
I reach out into empty space.
When I feel my sun-warmed wicker chair,
I find I am located.
I am home.

A Good Morning Shower Song

It so happens, my sweet,
we end up naked down to our feet,
one step, one step,
over the curb and we're in,
standing in a shower,
my bandaged right arm in a plastic bag.

I am unstable, blind, so recently sick, now injured,
you have to come along,
pressing your smaller body against mine
nudging me left, then right
across the slippery porcelain floor,
a neat trick. You soap me up,
guide the shower spray
over my head and shoulder
while I sit in the white plastic chair.

When I stand and reach out my hand
my pleasure is such that each random touch
of skin against skin is worthy of a kiss.
Such open-hearted joy
under the warming steam
as you hum a tune,
hose me down, rinse me clean,
leaving no crease or crevice unexplored.

What a gem of a morning routine
and a chance to enjoy my reward—
this unexpected sweetness—
my vulnerability dissipating,
released into the sauna and shower's heat.

Targeted Cancer Therapy

If God is God He is not good,
If God is good He is not God;
Take the even, take the odd,
I would not sleep here if I could
Except for the little green leaves in the wood
And the wind on the water.
        —J.B., *Archibald MacLeish*

The boat is always leaking
and time is all there is.

Steam rises and falls, dissipates,
reforms itself into the shape of a face
in the morning mirror. An assault begins.
I am scattered, still trapped in a sleep state
of images, dream faces.

Then I am aware of my physical body.
My body knows that I am a smoke-soaked
spiritual soup.
It wants to hold me together,
blood pumping,
pressure rising and falling,
breathing air,
standing upright
fighting spinal stenosis,
either part of a whole
or alone.

But my body can't.
My immune system weakens.
Targeted cancer therapy,
$500 a pill each day.
Still, the smoke of who I am
keeps dissipating, spiraling away.
Gravity can't hold it together.

It's not about gravity.
It's about reality states,
self or no-self.
I am either asleep or awake.
As I turn from the mirror
I know I am waking up,
taking one hesitating step at a time,
reaching out into emptiness
for the steadiness of the door jamb,
a secure place to stand
before beginning a new day.

Ode to Pneumonia

Darkling I listen; and, for many a time
  I have been half in love with easeful Death,
Call'd him soft names in many a mused rhyme,
  To take into the air my quiet breath
  —John Keats

At first, I think it's my tremor.
Then, I can't get warm: teeth chattering, body shaking.
My legs won't work.
The EMTs pick me up and put me on the stretcher.
I think I have a touch of pneumonia.
A light touch.

You've been around for a long time,
companion to sufferers of consumption.
But not this time, old friend, as I tell my wife.
The cold winter air four days before Christmas
brings me a surreal ride
down a long tunnel of traffic.

> The ER entrance is down stretches
> of curving dirt road, potholes, jolts, bumps.
> The cab of the ambulance separates
> from the box and goes on,
> the rest of it stays where it arrived.
> Gears grind,
> it becomes a room, filled with light,
> the stretcher becomes
> a table and then a bed.
> They try to start an IV,
> painful jabs,
> until a phlebotomist
> shows them
> how to find the vein.

The hospital convinces me the infection is serious.

They rig my bed with alarm bells
should I try to get out, which I do.
I don't know where I am.
Is there anything we can do for you?

I ask the nurses to shut off the strange beeping,
the vividness of its insistent repetition,
the anxiety of no control,
of being delivered into someone else's care,
of being a passive recipient,
of being unable to make it stop.

This morning, I think of Keats, his concept of
negative capability,
holding two opposing thoughts in your mind:

the end of things and the ending to things,
cessation, peace, release,
not beauty or truth, just a preview of things to come.

But say the word *pneumonia*,
echoes of the breath of God. Say it aloud.
It has a sweetness to it, like a cloud before the rain.
It could be a woman's name—Sonya, Fiona, Ramona—
a chance encounter on a street.
It could be a chaste yellow flower in a golden vase.

About Matej & Me

Matej comes into our bedroom, his voice bubbling up from his song book of beginning tunes, vowels and consonants. No words, just sound that decrescendos: an ear-piercing siren—an overheard ambulance or police car—down to imitations of his Tata and his Gammy Gail and me, his Papa.

I, of course, am just waking up, feeling every bit of my 81 years and his 18 months.

He picks up a bright object from a wobbly table covered with my medicines and eyedrops: a hand-powered, Russian-made flashlight. His mama shows him how to squeeze the lever to start the cogwheel spinning to light it up.

"Hah!" The friction of the teeth makes a sound that delights Matej. And me too, I must admit.
I am pleased by his bursts of joy, fueled by his curiosity and his love of sounds. His enjoyment and wonder at the things in the world are contagious. When Matej looks at a new object, he studies it first, approaching it carefully. *What is it?* Could be anything.

I pull myself up, leaning on my elbow, staring dimly across the 80-year gap between us.

It's true he brings chaos because his curiosity is attracted to any new object, particularly if he can pick it up. And then he puts it down anywhere as he goes on his way elsewhere. Gail, standing beside him as he turns to go, comments on his sturdy frame, his little legs and bottom.

He has few words, but he has a tune down—*ring, ring ring, banana phone, ring, ring ring, banana phone*—as he dances his way out of the room. *Papa, papa, papa, paaaapa, papaaaaa, papa.*

Matej's world is growing and mine is getting smaller.

Like him, I am trying to make myself understood. I practice sounds: forte to pianissimo, bass to baritone and back, holding my breath as long as I can, extending my range.

I am learning to move around in my house while nearly blind, to take advantage of what my Parkinson's allows, to enjoy the sensation of standing straight up (not bent over), not allowing my spinal stenosis to have its way with me for as long as I can, finding a new pleasure in taking a shower, the simple act of hot water, the sturdy comfort of my shower chair. The warm water electrifies, transforms loss of sensation in my fingertips and feet to tingling.

A simple hug of bodies touching: Matej is back.

He wants to climb in the bath right away, his water toys banging in the empty tub. We quickly fill it with warm water.

He splashes, immersed, while I sit in my chair under a spray. "Are we having a shower together?" I ask.

"No. Bub." *I'm in the shower and you're in the tub. It's different. Gotcha.* "Papa," he's reaching to give me my soap.

I turn off the shower. His mama, here with towels to dry us off, takes Matej from the tub.

He holds out a hand, touching me, says, "Papa hep." But I need an adult to hold my hands to step over the curb of the shower.

We are very much alike in what we take into our world and how we deal with the frustration of mastering what's possible. Matej has before him fields of enormous range, depth, and possibilities that are ever-increasing, as he learns to manage his senses, his hands able to grasp and hold.

Matej is learning to jump up. When he gets both feet off the ground, he applauds himself, throws his arms up in victory, beams at the world.

Meditation on Three Small Birds in Winter
A poem for my wife Gail

We look out the kitchen window.
There's a goldfinch in the tree,
two rose finches at the feeder.
I reach over, take your hand,
tell you *I love you.*
The rain begins pouring down
in torrents, sheets blown sideways,
from a new atmospheric river.
I think these birds are out of time,
a holdover from warmer weather.

We read Gene's two new poems,
sparking the connections between us,
floating *in the canoe of your singing voice,*
as we stare out at the ocean in Bodega Bay
and a view of myself
that makes me reevaluate my place.

We have a choice.
There are no excuses.
You are what you do
or what you don't do,
the author of all the choices you make.
You constructed this picture of yourself
and it's either honorable
or an ego-driven fiction of who you are.
It's really hard to know the difference.

I tell you I need to take charge of my life
so I know what I'm doing
when I let go of it, give it up.

My life force feels punctured.
Change is coming. There is an
arterial insufficiency.

It's hard to see around
this fact of who we were.
I recall the trilling of the goldfinch and you.
It sustains me as I think about my life
and who I have been
with you and the world as we knew it.

"Gail and Charles in a Duet" and
"Conversing with Charles" *(2022)*,
Gene Berson

In Transit

*...being lost really means we're in transit... moving from where
we were to an eventual place of where we will soon be.*
—Marisa Donnelly

*"[L]ost" comes from the Old Norse los, meaning the disbanding of an
army... falling out of formation to go home, a truce with the wide world.*
—Rebecca Solnit

I.

It's still dark,
no light coming in through the window.
You know where you are,
but you are also lost.
The ribbon in your hand
leads to the next room.
You are not lost.

Your feet hit the floor.
Your right leg
does not want to support you.
You want to say
this is your Parkinson's taking charge,
but it's not.

The instability of your life threatens your equilibrium.
Move carefully lest you fall.

The gas pilot clicks, the floor shudders, the heat exhales on.
Your wife sighs deeply in the night.

Where are you going?
You do not know.
You have been here before.
There is more to be explored,
but you are disassembling.

You are like water.
You need to move to stay alive.
You want to go forward,
but to where is not clear.

Your brain is a prediction machine.
It matches your expectations to your perceptions.
But it's not working right.
You want to surrender, join with the night,
give in to quiescence, follow the rhythm,
retreat into sleep.

II.

What am I doing holding a ribbon,
small careful steps in the dark,
thinking about my friend
lost in space and time,
having had a massive stroke?

He was on a guided psilocybin trip.
When he returned, I was going to go next.
Was he aware when it happened?
Was he going into the next room?
If he comes back, will he return
with some beautiful dream?
He was searching for an absolute truth.
It was unbelievable, I heard he said.

When you are unconscious, you are nowhere.
What happens to the prediction machine?
Is it unprepared for the surprise of the unknown?

The second stroke wiped out what remained,
startling; he is no longer on this planet.
The Tom I knew is lost,
not in this world, not anywhere:
letting me take his arm,
guiding me from one place to another,

talking with me
when I felt washed ashore and isolated,
his bellowing laughter ringing through my hallway,
his mindfulness, his secular form of Buddhism,
his sense of peace and goodwill
spread before us like a prepared meal.

I am thinking about what it means to be dead.
Maybe we return to the beginning of all life:
no self, just invented stories,
living in the world but not entangling with it,
a goal-less goal, a form of awakening.

III.

I open my eyes and feel
like I have changed the channel.
It is still dark, yet I can see
unreal faces, sad-eyed masquerade masks
on the wall before me,
observing. I close my eyes.
The faces are still there.
I am more comfortable in my inner world
than the world of doors and dressers.

I don't know where I am going,
but I am going, even though it is dark.
I hold onto the ribbon that will lead me to the next room
where I must let go and find my way
on my own, alone.

Migration

I am standing on our whale rock, a granite outcropping in the backyard, looking down a thousand feet and one hundred years into the South Yuba River Valley, above a skein of black- and-white snow geese flying northward in the distance, following the contour of the canyon. I know the river is running far below. This evening the flow of rushing water is reaching my ear.

In an instant the flock banks, an avalanche of white, and disappears into a cloud, only to return a moment later as they finish their turn: rising and falling, becoming visible and invisible, navigating chinooks, flying into the gusts of wind. It's magical to see them floating, shimmering in an October light, a hallowed happening whether I'm here to see it or not.

I feel privileged and honored to witness this journey at the end of a seasonal pattern–a reckoning that all of life begins and ends–so that dying is one more door in living. It occurs to me that the flock is following the river upstream to a resting place. They rise to cross the mountain range, a blizzard of white light, not to reappear again in my sight, sailing silently then becoming loud and voluble as they disappear, the eerie honking sound still in my ear.

It makes me think of migration patterns, years in development, and the end of all that. The future suddenly empty and blank. Not suddenly. Empty of plans, oversight, or control. And I want to go with the birds as they ascend into invisibility.

fin.

Grateful acknowledgment:

to the editors of these magazines where these poems or earlier versions of them first appeared:

"On Going Blind," *US1 Worksheets*, May 2023; *Louisville Review,* 2019; "Gratitude," "Acknowledging Parkinson's," *Louisville Review*, 2019;

to members of our terrific Writers' Workshop:

Judy Bebelaar, Eugene Berson, Demian Entrekin, Gail Entrekin, Stewart Florsheim, Grace Grafton, Leah Korican, and Scott Young;

to Gail, who suffers with me all the indignities of my diseases

to Luke, fellow writer, editor, philosopher, and longtime friend;

to Heidi, without whose help this work would not be possible.

Hip Pocket Press Mission Statement

It is our belief that the arts are the embodiment of the soul of a culture, that the promotion of writers and artists is essential if our current culture, with its emphasis on media and provocative outcomes, is to have a chance to develop that inner voice and ear that expresses and listens to beauty. Toward that end, Hip Pocket Press will continue to search out and discover poets and writers whose voices can give us a clearer understanding of ourselves and of the culture which defines us.

Other Books From Hip Pocket Press

Café Dissertation: D. James Smith (poetry)

Storyland: Keith Dunlap (poetry)

The Occasionist: Curt Anderson (poetry)

Jester: Grace Marie Grafton (poetry)

The Berkeley Poets Cooperative: A History of the Times:
    Charles Entrekin, Editor (essays)

Even That Indigo: John Smith (poetry)

Ex Vivo (Out of the Living Body): Kirsten Casey (poetry)

The More Difficult Beauty: Molly Fisk (poetry)

Yuba Flows: Kirsten Casey, Gary Cooke, Cheryl Dumesnil, Judy Halebsky,
    Iven Lourie, & Scott Young; Gail Rudd Entrekin, Editor (poetry)

Songs for a Teenage Nomad: Kim Culbertson (young adult fiction)

Truth Be Told: Tom Farber (epigrams)

Sierra Songs & Descants: Poetry & Prose of the Sierra:
    Gail Rudd Entrekin, Editor

A Common Ancestor: Marilee Richards (poetry)

Terrain: Dan Bellm, Molly Fisk, Forrest Hamer (poetry)

You Notice the Body: Gail Rudd Entrekin (poetry)

Web Publications

Canary, a Literary Journal of the Environmental Crisis:
    Gail Rudd Entrekin, Editor
Sisyphus, Essays on Language, Culture & the Arts:
    Charles Entrekin, Heidi Varian & Luke Wallin, Editors

About This Book: Why It Is Self-Published

Hip Pocket Press (HPP) evolved out of The Berkeley Poets Workshop & Press, which represented decades of my literary life. What were we doing? As a cooperative, we were providing writing workshops, free and open to the public; we were providing a forum within the Berkeley community for the exchange of ideas, for criticism and support for the writing process; we were promoting poetry as a viable art form; we were publishing it, giving it the dignity of print; and we were having a say in what counts as literature in America.

Susan Stern of *The Daily Cal* said of the workshops and the magazines we produced, "The magazine represents the best work to come out of the weekly poetry workshops, where anyone is invited to come, read their poetry, discuss their work with other poets, criticize others' work, drink too much coffee and inevitably disrupt things a little by crawling over everyone in search of the bathroom… If you come to it you become it…."

Today, my physical limitations make it impossible for me to go off and promote this book, so I feel that I can't ask HPP to bear the costs of publication of a book that can't be promoted by the full capacity of the press. Rather than participate in the editorial process, I chose these poems myself, and I am publishing this chapbook. These poems are an expression of my current process: how cancer left me immunocompromised in a pandemic, and Parkinson's disease has created "waking dreams." Glaucoma, which would seem to be the least dangerous, has cost me the most. I can't read nor write nor drive a car nor play tennis nor do anything to enjoy the full spectrum of what life has to offer, so I remain indebted to the poetic process to find life's significance, learning to embrace what remains.

In his new collection, Charles Entrekin confronts and illuminates his journey into darkness and debilitating illness. Among his losses he discovers unexpected tenderness, gratitude and joy, as his senses enlarge and his awareness deepens. When a barista helps him with his phone, he says "I am so/ grateful I want to cry." And later, "The clutter falls away... (I am) discovering the being I am becoming."

Entrekin describes the emotional landscape of illness in vivid detail. Of Parkinson's he writes, "The tremor/is like a squirrel crossing the road/indecisive, running left, then right." And when he falls ill with pneumonia, "But say the word pneumonia,/echoes of the breath of God. Say it aloud./It has a sweetness to it, like a cloud before the rain."

He offers us impeccably crafted poems in language that is both conversational and rich with detail. This is a life-affirming book: honest, courageous and true.

—GAIL NEWMAN, *Blood Memory*

Charles Entrekin's newest book of poems is an act of courage. With depth and insight, by showing compassion and tenderness for his declining body, he enables his readers to accept—indeed, to embrace—the inevitability of our own mortality with honesty and forgiveness. These poems form the steps he employs to come to grips with blindness and the multiple diseases invading his body—to remain aware and vigorously alive, as he approaches this "threshold."

—GRACE GRAFTON, *Jester*

With courage and skillful transparency, Charles Entrekin locates, through lyric, story, and philosophical questions, our common ground as humans: "When all we have/ is this fragile appreciation/ of a willingness/ to love and be loved/, when whatever we have/ we hold between us." These poems by Charles Entrekin are a generous and resonant invitation to us to notice our lives beyond our expectations, to be present in the time we have: "Grateful to taste …Grateful for the words …Grateful to visit with friends/ while the present disappears."

—CARTER MCKENZIE, *Stem of Us*

Printed in the USA
CPSIA information can be obtained
at www.ICGtesting.com
CBHW020008220324
5653CB00012B/739